THE COFFEE MEDITATIONS

30 Lessons From Coffee to Brew a Life of Growth, Clarity, and Success

Lucas Almonte

212
PUBLISHING

ISBN 979-8-9999973-3-3 (paperback)
ISBN 979-8-9999973-1-9 (hardcover)
ISBN 979-8-9999973-0-2 (eBook)
Library of Congress Control Number: 2025919757

Publication Date: October 1, 2025 (International Coffee Day)

Illustrations and images used under license from Shutterstock.com

212 Publishing, LLC
New York, NY

www.thecoffeemeditations.com

CONTENTS

To my mom, Laly –
from humble grounds, to full cup.
This brew is for you.

INTRODUCTION

This book is for the busy professional who may be overwhelmed with work or unsure of their path, the thoughtful person who wants to find more profound significance in everyday moments, and the coffee lover who craves more than just the caffeine rush from their daily cup. It is for those who believe they can achieve greater growth, clarity, and success in their lives. I know because I wrote this book for myself.

When I started this journey, I was only a few months into my career as a freshly minted attorney back home in New York City when the COVID-19 lockdown began. Like many others, I found the lockdown to be disorienting. I found myself trying to make sense of the new lifestyle and searching for a new rhythm. Out of simple necessity, I started making my own coffee at home more frequently.

What started as an attempt to brew a tastier cup of coffee soon evolved into a deep dive into the intricate world of coffee and the variables involved in making it, such as grind size, extraction, water chemistry, and milk texture. But this technical exploration took on deeper meaning when I learned about my family's direct connection with coffee through my mom's stories. My mom grew up on a small farm in the rural mountains of the Dominican Republic, where she would pick coffee cherries by hand and roast coffee beans at home. It was then that I understood that this journey was more than just learning how to make coffee. In those lessons and in the quiet routine, I noticed patterns that mirrored life itself. Over time, coffee became a helpful lens through which I reflected on deeper concepts, such as growth, purpose, discipline, and success.

However, since then, the concept for this book had been brewing in my imagination, lacking form and focus. It was only when I started to see the signs of burnout in my life over the last two years that those lessons came to the forefront of my mind. As I thought about how to organize my ideas and write this book, I kept going back to a book I read for the first time over a summer break more than ten years ago:

Marcus Aurelius's *Meditations*. Marcus Aurelius, a Roman emperor, wrote *Meditations* over 2,000 years ago to remind him of the principles and perspectives he wanted to guide his life.

I first read *Meditations* during a period of uncertainty in my life. In February 2012, I enlisted in the United States Army after dropping out of college. However, a few weeks before the start of boot camp, I was disqualified from service due to a recently diagnosed chronic medical condition, which I had only become aware of after feeling sick during a pre-boot camp training session. The eight years I had committed to service were quickly disrupted by the disqualification, leaving me searching for a new path and a structure to ground my thoughts and next steps. In *Meditations*, I found insights and wisdom that helped me remain calm during times of uncertainty. Although reading *Meditations* did not erase the challenges I faced, it provided me with greater clarity to view the uncertainty from a different perspective.

Framework

Meditations is structured as a compilation of fragmented reminders and reflections. For this book, however, I wanted to take a different approach and instead discuss each idea further in order to properly trace the connection between coffee and life. As I continued to reflect on how to structure this book, I recalled that the ancient Greek philosopher Aristotle argued in his *Posterior Analytics* that we come to know universal truths by first understanding the particulars. This insight helped me recognize the path I was already following. Learning about coffee taught me *particular* lessons that applied only to the craft of coffee, such as how to roast beans, control the water flow, and steam milk for latte art. But, as I reflected on those *particular* lessons, they revealed *universal* truths about patience, preparedness, balance, and growth that apply to life. It was through this process of moving from the specific to the universal that my meditations and reflections took shape.

Many of the reflections shared here originated from the notes I kept in my dedicated coffee notebook (basically a compendium) during the pandemic. Those contemporaneous notes and reflections became the foundation from which this book took shape. As part of my process to extract and refine ideas from my notebook into this book, I applied the following framework:

Observation + Intention → Insight

First, I observed *what* I was doing or learning about (for example, weighing the beans, controlling the amount of pressure, and cleaning my equipment). Then, I tried to understand *why* that particular action or concept was important (for example, learning to control the variables helps the extraction of coffee be more consistent). This formula led to a specific understanding of coffee, which I then attempted to connect with broader insights applicable to life. These broader insights eventually became the meditations that open each chapter in this book.

When I finally sat down to write, it felt like—borrowing an idea from Michelangelo—chiseling away at a block of murky marble until the shape inside began to emerge. This book represents the sculpture that was inside the marble. What started as observations while making coffee gradually revealed broader truths about life through deep reflection and intentional refinement. The same method that helped me extract these insights can also help you navigate other aspects of life. Aristotle's principle of moving from the specific to the general reminds us that clarity often begins with paying attention to the details. When we pay close attention to what we are doing and the intentions behind our choices, we begin to notice patterns that reveal the principles guiding our lives. And when we examine these principles, we create space to choose how we truly want to live.

What You Should Expect

I tried to avoid coffee-related topics that were too complicated or technical, but my thoughts are based on a mix of observations, science, analogies, and puns. Although a basic familiarity with coffee practices or knowledge may enrich the reflections, it's not required. Like a good cup of coffee, I hope the insights in this book are accessible and enjoyable for everyone.

Please also note that this book is not intended to be a collection of quick, self-help fixes. It is also not meant to be a declaration of my mastery of coffee or, for that matter, life. Like Marcus Aurelius, I wrote this book to help me remember these principles, which I often forget. These meditations and reflections are just as much for me as they are for you. Although I won't always embody the clarity or consistency of the principles discussed here, this book is part of my lifelong practice.

How to Use This Book

This book, like *Meditations*, can be read straight through in sequence or in any order. As noted, this book differs from *Meditations* in its structure. Instead of a list of short, standalone insights, each chapter in this book is precisely one page in length, focusing on a single coffee-related topic. There are about 300-350 words in each chapter, which should take you a few minutes to read, or just enough time to drink your coffee! In particular, each chapter has:

- A meditation (a high-level insight extracted from my reflections).
- A section for my reflections and coffee-related knowledge, which may help you further understand the topic discussed in that chapter.
- A "Brew On These" section with questions to help you think more deeply about the lessons and integrate them into your everyday life. Spend some time brewing on these questions. The purpose here is to push yourself to reflect deeply and honestly.

In total, the core of this book is divided into three parts, each comprising 10 chapters. Part I focuses on the cycle of growth and transformation. Although each chapter can be read independently of the others, I structured Part I to follow the life cycle of coffee, from planting to harvesting, drying, roasting, and grinding. Part II is about preparing to achieve success in life while focusing on the tools and steps needed to make a good cup of coffee. Part III focuses on crafting a meaningful and purposeful life by examining the process of making a cup of coffee, savoring it, and exploring beyond.

At the end of this book, you'll find the following five additional sections that may help you better understand and apply the lessons in your daily life:

1. *"The Practice"* – This section brings together all of the meditations from each chapter in a simple table format so you can quickly review them together.
2. *"Behind the Brew"* – This section provides a brief look at my creative process, focusing on how the thinking, writing, cover design, and curation all came together to form this book.
3. *"Further Reading"* – This section offers a list of books worth exploring if you wish to continue this journey of self-reflection, growth, and mindful living beyond this book.
4. *"The Language of Coffee"* – This section contains a glossary, along with a bibliography, of the key coffee-related terms and definitions used in this book and other key words.
5. Blank Pages – I've also included some blank, lined pages for you to write down your thoughts, notes, and reflections as you read.

I hope this book will provide you with new perspectives and the simple practices needed to put them into action every day, just as they continue to remind me to do the same. Perhaps the next time you make coffee at home or visit a coffee shop, you will notice some of the ideas discussed here and develop a greater appreciation for your coffee, and, more importantly, life.

This page is an intentional pause . . .

savor the present moment.

PART I

The Growth & Transformation Cycle

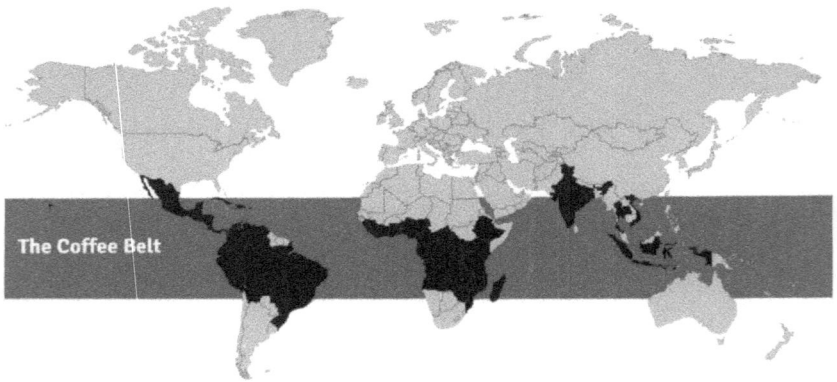

The Coffee Belt

THE RIGHT ENVIRONMENT

Be mindful of the environments where you choose to grow.

Most of the world's coffee is grown in an area known as the "coffee belt," which spans about 23.5 degrees north to 23.5 degrees south of the equator. In this zone, the steady rainfall, climate, and mineral-rich soil align to create optimal conditions for coffee plants to thrive. Even though the coffee belt reflects ideal conditions, it's the individual farms and plots where the coffee plants grow that give the beans their distinct flavors and determine their quality. For example, other crops that grow near coffee plants can alter the mineral balance in the soil or create unwanted shade over the coffee plants, which may deprive the coffee plants of the light they need to grow. As a result, the development of the coffee plants, and ultimately the flavors of the coffee, are altered.

Like coffee plants, we are transformed by the conditions of our environment. The places where we live and grow shape who we become, just as different farms grow coffee beans with different flavors. Our thoughts, actions, and development are influenced by the people we surround ourselves with, the physical and digital spaces where we spend our time, and what we consume. While you couldn't choose where you were raised, you can choose where you grow from here. To create the best conditions for you to flourish today, identify and change the elements in your environment that are holding you back and lean into those elements that support your development. Even the smallest shifts in your environment can have a significant impact on who you become.

Brew On These:
- What does your "coffee belt" look like? Are there certain places, groups of people, or practices that can better help you grow?
- Are you choosing places that help you grow, or are you hoping to thrive in environments that are unsuitable for you? What changes can you make to your environment to help you thrive?

CULTIVATING PATIENCE

To be patient does not imply doing nothing. Being patient means being in harmony with nature and trusting the process without demanding an immediate reward.

It can take three to four years for new coffee plants to produce their first fruits, known as *"cherries,"* and then several more months for those cherries to be ready for harvesting. In that period, the coffee plants may experience seasons of drought, extreme heat, flood, and frost before they flourish. And yet, the coffee farmer has to trust the process and do their best to care for the plants. Farmers know that trying to speed up the growth and maturity of the coffee plants will only lead to bitterness and disappointment.

Like the best coffees, our character develops with time and care. If we rush our growth, we can end up with a character that is as disappointing as unripe coffee cherries: not fully developed, bitter, and lacking depth. We also can't let other people's impatience affect how we grow. Each season of adversity strengthens us, and yet those seasons are often unseen or unappreciated by others. What appears to be dormancy to others is often the work that goes on behind the scenes to make us more resilient, just as the farmer knows that coffee plants need to build resilience and strong roots below the surface before they can fully develop and produce. Ultimately, we need to learn to cultivate excellence by being patient and devoted to the process, rather than rushing it. It is okay if you do not thrive right away or in every season. You will thrive when you are ready.

Brew On These:
- Do you allow yourself the patience to grow, or do you rush results before their time?
- Where in your life do you confuse being still with being stuck? Are you more focused on demonstrating your growth to others or on truly becoming more grounded for the next phase?

PRECISION OVER SPEED

It is not the quantity of experiences that shapes you most deeply, but the care with which you approach those moments. How you harvest life's moments reflects what you value most.

The two most common methods of harvesting coffee cherries are hand-picking and machine harvesting. Hand-picking allows the harvester to carefully select only the ripe, high-quality cherries, leaving the unripe cherries on the tree to mature. With machine harvesting, however, the harvester can shake the coffee tree and quickly collect all the cherries, even the unripe ones. Each method has its own benefits and trade-offs compared to the other. While mechanized harvesting prioritizes quantity and speed, hand-picking emphasizes precision through careful selection and the intimacy of human touch, though at the expense of speed. But a harvester's choice of which approach to use depends on factors like the type of terrain (flat land or rough), the availability of skilled workers or expensive machinery, the crop size, and the goals of the business.

Life also offers us opportunities to choose between approaching experiences with care and precision or rushing through them. When we engage with each moment deliberately by pausing to reflect and internalize what we learned, we gain a profound insight and lasting development. But if we move too fast from one experience to the next, checking off a list rather than absorbing meaning, we risk overlooking the richness and wisdom of each moment. Like harvesting coffee cherries, the quality of the experiences we harvest depends on the approach we choose.

Brew On These:
- Are you prioritizing quality over quantity in the things you do and the decisions you make?
- How would your life change if you treated each day with the same care and intention of a hand-picked harvest? What things would you leave behind that are not yet ready to be harvested?

SORTING AND LETTING GO WITH PURPOSE

Not everything that grows with you is meant to continue with you.
Part of growth is learning to release what no longer serves you so you can carry
forward only what aligns with your values and purpose.

Once coffee cherries are harvested and collected, they are sorted by quality before being processed. Although a coffee cherry may have shown promise at the time of picking, that alone does not mean it must continue to the final product. Ripeness and maturity are subtle and nuanced traits that extend beyond the appearance of the cherries. Some of the harvested coffee cherries will not meet the standard for a specific batch of coffee. A common method of quality control is the "floating test," where cherries are submerged in water. The unripe or defective cherries float to the top, known as *"floaters,"* while the developed cherries sink. The floaters are set aside for other uses, allowing only the best and most promising cherries to be used for premium batches. But to know which cherries to keep, farmers need to be clear about what kind of coffee product they want to produce and let go of anything that does not align with their vision, allowing them to focus on what will help them achieve their goals.

Life calls for the same level of care and meticulous approach. Just as unripe or defective cherries are set aside to maintain the quality of the batch, we must also discard any thoughts, habits, or beliefs that do not align with our vision and purpose. By clearing away what weighs us down, we create space to invest only in what truly matters and prevent the bitter from blending in and spoiling the sweetness of life.

Brew On These:
- What thoughts, habits, or relationships are you holding on to without checking if they truly support your growth?
- Do you trust yourself to release what no longer serves you or meets your standards, even if it used to be important to you?

METHODS OF MATURATION

It is not just that we endure, but how we endure that determines the depth of who we become.

After processing, coffee beans are dried using one of three main drying methods: natural, washed, or honey. Each of these methods resembles a different path to personal growth and maturation. The natural process leaves whole coffee cherries to dry slowly in the sun, preserving all their natural characteristics and flaws intact. The washed process strips away the cherry's outer layers to reveal the raw beans, much like how we shed excess layers to reveal our true character. After this step, the beans are washed to remove any remaining layers, known as "*mucilage*," and then dried in the sun. The honey method is a mix of both the natural and washed methods. It removes the outer layers (similar to the washed method) but retains the interior mucilage, which binds with the beans during drying to make them taste sweeter. However, no single method is superior to another; it all depends on which characteristics the farmers want to highlight.

In the same way, we develop on different paths. Some people are transformed slowly, through repeated exposure to situations that shape them over time. Others are transformed suddenly when they experience an unexpected event that changes them profoundly with force. Both paths reveal depth but in different ways. In the end, what matters most is not whether your transformation journey was long and gentle or sudden and severe, but whether you can recognize and understand how it has transformed you. In that recognition, what we experience and how we experience it becomes wisdom for us to carry in life.

Brew On These:
- Which of your transformations have had the most significant impact on you? Which of these transformations unfolded slowly, and which happened quickly? How has each path added a different depth to your character?

UNCONVENTIONAL METHODS, PROFOUND RESULTS

Do not fear the unfamiliar path. Growth often requires us to reject old methods that no longer serve us.

Nature evolves on its own, but sometimes we need to go against both nature and tradition to become a better version of ourselves. Even if traditional methods of drying coffee beans are still the most commonly used, new methods, such as anaerobic fermentation and carbonic maceration, are pushing the limits of coffee's flavors beyond what traditional methods can produce. These two experimental methods, borrowed from the wine industry, involve placing whole coffee cherries (for carbonic maceration) or depulped coffee beans (for anaerobic fermentation) in sealed containers without oxygen, along with some spices or fruits, to produce bright and unique flavor profiles.

Just as co-fermented coffee beans develop their complex flavors through intentional isolation, a significant change occurs within us when we take the time and space to evolve away from the eyes of others. In those quiet depths of solitude, when we are cut off from the outside world and the pressure of the public spotlight, we can sit with our deepest truths, face our contradictions, and undergo a subtle transformation. Through this process of self-reflection, our perception of ourselves is altered, and we emerge with a depth and complexity of character that was unexpected. So, like with co-fermented coffee, don't be afraid to try new things and stray from the standard. Have the courage to abandon the old way of doing things and explore unconventional paths that will shape your unique character.

Brew On These:
- Have you dismissed a method or path simply because it looked unfamiliar? In what areas of your life are you afraid to experiment?
- What conditions in your life feel uncomfortable now but might be fermenting a deeper version of yourself that you do not yet understand or appreciate?

FROM RAW TO READY

Avoiding challenges means remaining raw, undeveloped, and untested.
The heat of the challenges we fear is often what we need to reveal our essence.

The high temperatures of roasting make the raw, green coffee beans fracture and expand. The heat that would burn and ruin other substances instead refines coffee beans, unlocking their hidden depth, aroma, and flavors. But no two beans emerge from the same heat with the same results. Each variety of coffee has its own distinct characteristics that react differently to the roast. Some beans reveal bright acidity and fruity notes when lightly roasted, while others reveal deep chocolate and earthy flavors when exposed to prolonged heat. But if you roast certain beans for too long, they will lose their best features. The most important thing is to understand how each type of bean reacts.

Challenges in life, like the heat in the roaster, also transform us. If we shy away from challenges, we risk remaining raw, unchanged, and full of untapped potential. The heat of the challenges we face in life may be unpleasant and discomforting. Yet, it's often necessary to burn away our impurities and unleash a more refined version of ourselves. During extended periods of challenges, we are forced to tap into our reserves of resilience and determination, uncovering our true potential and developing depth of character. But we all respond differently to the challenges life throws at us, just like how different kinds of coffee beans react differently to the same fire. Transformation is not meant to make us all the same. It's meant to unlock the distinct notes of our characters. And the longer the roast, the deeper and richer the transformation. Just remember not to burn yourself out along the way!

Brew On These:
- What parts of you are still raw and fresh, and how can you apply the right kind of heat to grow without burning what matters most?
- How do you distinguish between challenges that are refining you and those that are burning you out?

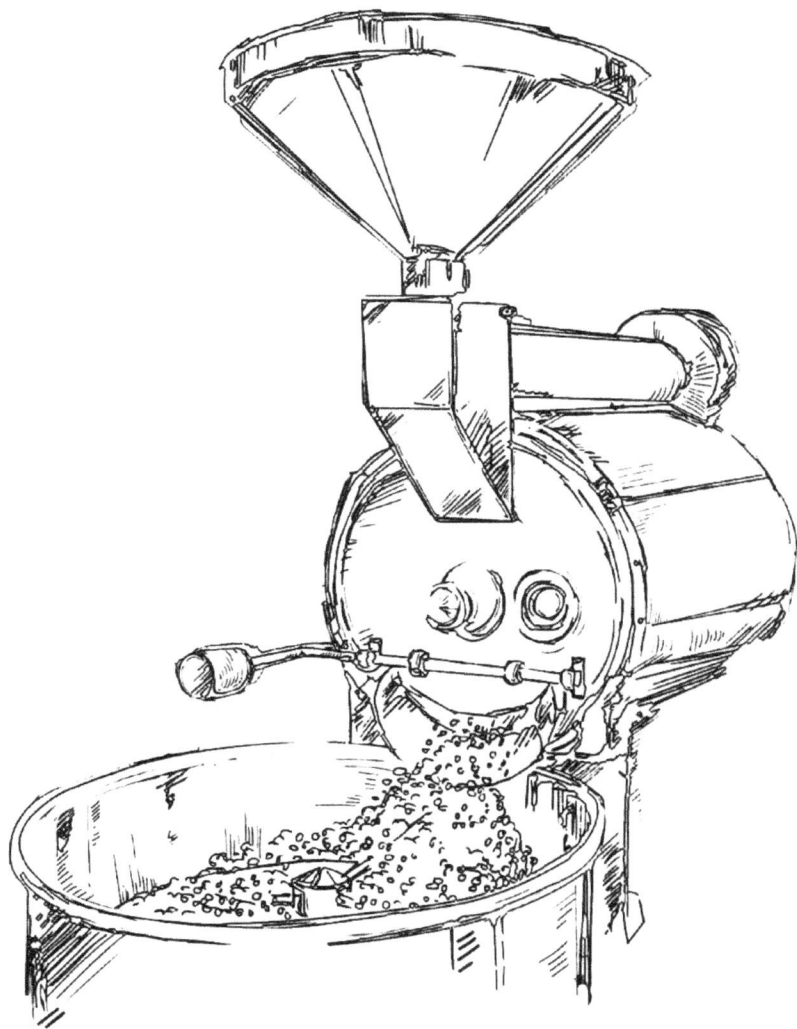

TRANSFORMATION REQUIRES INTEGRATION

*To be transformed means not just to change but also to absorb the change.
After any transformation, take a moment to pause and align yourself with the
changes you experienced.*

Freshly roasted coffee beans are alive with an intense aroma, but their full flavor potential is not yet fully realized. At this stage, the beans carry both the mark of transformation from the roast and the tension of what still needs time to settle. When coffee beans are roasted, the intense heat triggers a series of chemical reactions that not only draw out and develop flavor but also produce carbon dioxide and other gases that become trapped within the bean. Because of these trapped gases, the coffee beans need to rest for a few weeks after roasting to allow all the gases to slowly release before they can be ground and brewed (this process is referred to as "*de-gassing*"). If you brew too soon after roasting, the trapped gases will interfere with the extraction and make the coffee taste disappointing. This intentional pause to de-gas is not inaction; it's an important step for the beans to release what is no longer useful and settle into their true essence.

When we are undergoing a transformation, there is an impulse to act and capitalize on the momentum. However, in doing so, we still carry old energy that needs to be released before we can move forward. Transformation is a process, and we need to pause after each transformation to allow us to integrate the lessons and align ourselves with our new version. In taking the time to calibrate ourselves, we remember where we have been and where we are meant to go, and we can go even further if we de-gas ourselves from any old energy. But if we act too soon, we risk letting the lack of depth and clarity interfere with a life of richness and purpose.

Brew On These:
- In the rush to keep moving, what hasn't settled since your last big change in your life? How could taking a break help you release things that don't need to remain trapped inside you anymore?

UNIFIED, NOT UNIFORM

Character is not born from uniformity, but from the careful blending of opposing elements into something richer than their parts.

When creating new coffee blends, the roaster looks for contrasts, not similarity. For instance, the bright, citrus notes of Ethiopian beans may find a perfect complement in the chocolatey depth of Colombian beans. The floral lightness of one origin tempers the bold earthiness of another. Each variety of coffee contributes qualities that the others cannot produce on their own. The final blend transcends the individual varieties of coffee. This is the paradox of excellence: harmony requires difference, much like a mosaic requires varied colors and tiles to form an image.

The same goes for life. Real personal growth often arises from friction, which is sometimes found in contradicting thoughts, competing desires, or seemingly incompatible experiences. For example, the bright notes of joy balance out the dark roast of hardship. When we ignore tension or try to make everything the same, our character stays limited, flat, and one-dimensional. But growth doesn't always mean eliminating these tensions. Sometimes it means knowing how to keep opposing forces or experiences in the right order. This harmony lets each element temper and strengthen the other. When we learn to harmonize the different aspects of ourselves and our circumstances, we become more unified and unique. To lead a deep and harmonious life, remember to carefully combine diverse experiences and knowledge, just as different types of beans are blended to create a complex and balanced coffee.

Brew On These:
- What attributes that used to seem like opposites have become your most significant source of strength or clarity?
- How do you choose which parts to add to your character and which parts to leave out? What standards are you applying to make the version of yourself that you want to be?

LIFE'S DAILY GRIND

Change doesn't always arrive gently. Sometimes change destroys what
we thought was permanent, not to punish us, but to prepare us
for a deeper purpose.

When coffee beans surrender to the grinder, the strong vortex created in the grinder crushes the hard shells of the beans. But this crushing force can also be viewed as an act of liberation. The burrs of the grinder free the beans from their shells, which are not useful for their next phase. Isn't this how we grow? There are times in life when things happen that break down our defenses and leave us exposed in our most vulnerable state. Like coffee beans, we are not meant to stay the same as we were before. Just as we cannot unlock the flavors of coffee beans without breaking them, we also cannot reach our potential without first letting go of our current selves to become who we could be. The unavoidable friction of existence grinds down our egos and transforms us into a new form so that we can become whole in the process.

Our refinement from one form to another also depends on how willing we are to face and trust the burrs of life that refine us. Although it's easy to resent the crushing pressures of life and instead demand immediate transformation, resisting the grind keeps us in our current state and hampers our ability to evolve. In the midst of destruction and chaos exists the essence of change and creation. So, remember to meet life's challenges like how coffee beans meet the burrs of the grinder: not with resistance, but with faith that what is truest in you will be revealed. The grind exists to free us from our current version and shape us into who we are meant to become.

Brew On These:
- How might holding on to who you are now make it harder to reach your goal?
- What do you need to change and refine about yourself today to better align with the path you are meant to take next in life?

This page is an intentional pause . . .

let the noise fade.

PART II

Preparing for Success & The Tools to Achieve It

RESPECT THE HIDDEN ORDER OF SUCCESS

No matter how small the task, the quality of the outcome is determined by the care and mindfulness with which we approach it.

Making a good cup of coffee requires a specific order of steps. Just as the initial preparation steps (such as selecting the beans and grinding them) set the stage for the cup we make, our choices and actions in life dictate the course of what comes next. It would not make sense to add whole coffee beans to the coffeepot without first grinding them. While our coffee routine may already be subconsciously ingrained in our minds, disregarding it invites bitterness into our cup and chaos into our souls. Each step in making coffee builds upon the foundation of the previous steps. When done with care, these steps result in a delicious cup of coffee.

The same holds true in our pursuit of success. Hard work alone may not pay off if we ignore the order that governs success. True success demands discipline and measured steps that build upon one another and carry us forward. However, before we can take any steps, we must first clarify our intentions and establish the foundations. Growth without reflection, action without preparation, or ambition without alignment all lead to imbalance, much like how tamping coffee grounds that aren't properly distributed or balanced produces an uneven extraction and a bitter result.

Brew On These:
- When results disappoint, do you reflect on the subtle order you may have ignored?
- What quality of attention do you give each moment, and how does it affect what follows?

TOOLS FOR SUCCESS

True readiness is less about the number of tools you have and more about having the wisdom to choose and apply them right. Even the right tool that is misapplied becomes the wrong choice.

Each tool we use to prepare our coffee plays a unique role and serves a distinct purpose: the grinder determines consistency, the distribution tool's fine needles gently break apart clumps of ground coffee, the scale ensures balance, and the gooseneck kettle offers control over the pour. You can't use these tools interchangeably, and it's difficult to use them effectively without knowing how they work. If you ignore the scale or use the wrong grinder setting, the entire extraction will be thrown off.

In our case, virtues are the instruments of the soul, each designed to serve a particular purpose. However, when misapplied, as when wielding truth without compassion or justice without mercy, they can cause chaos and imbalance. To prepare for success, remember that not all problems are solved through force. Some require quick action, while others require patience. Tools, like virtues, are neutral until they are applied to tasks that align with their intended purpose. Ultimately, wisdom isn't about having the most tools or the most knowledge. Wisdom is about knowing when, why, and how to use what we know. Like making a good cup of coffee, success comes from careful planning, measured effort, and the discipline to use the tools that serve our goals. When we align our virtues with our life goals, we create the conditions for extracting the most out of life.

Brew On These:
- Are you grinding hard trying to reach a goal using a method or instrument that was never meant for the job?
- Which simple virtue might you have overlooked as ordinary, yet could transform your soul more deeply if you learned to apply it correctly or with greater precision?

THE RIGHT VESSEL

Not every cup is made to hold every brew. Preparing for success starts with choosing what fits not just in form but also in purpose. What looks right at first may not necessarily serve who you are becoming.

The cup we choose shapes our experience with our coffee. Some cups are aesthetically pleasing but functionally hard to drink from. The shape of the rim may sit awkwardly against our lips, or the handles may be incorrectly placed or sized, making the grip uncomfortable. Some cups are made of materials, like glass or metal, that do not retain heat well, become too hot to handle when hot coffee is poured inside, or alter the coffee's flavor. Yet, how often do we choose the familiar cup or the cup closest to us without first considering if the properties of that cup align with the type of coffee we plan to drink?

Our most important vessel in life is not a ceramic mug. It's the mind. The properties of our minds shape our experience with life, and like a well-made cup, our minds need to be prepared to hold what matters. A mind that is cracked loses focus, and a mind cluttered with distractions, ego, or compulsions distorts how we perceive things and how we make decisions. It is not enough to have a large cup or an expansive mind to determine how much or what we can carry. A mind that is unfit for the task of personal growth and success will slow our progress and cloud our judgment. That is why it's important to be mindful of the ideas we entertain, the distractions we release, and the mindset we develop. In doing so, we prepare our minds as vessels to carry and guide us forward on the journey of growth and success.

Brew On These:
- What cracks in your mindset might be draining your momentum?
- Are you putting significant effort into something that can't hold it and then wondering why the heat of your vision fades so quickly?

THE WEIGHT OF PRECISION

Before action, weigh. Before weighing, pause and reset. Before resetting, begin with clarity of intent.

Precision holds power. An excellent cup of coffee is not just a reflection of the quality of the beans, water, or equipment used. It's also about the precision and intention applied while making the coffee. Before the first drop of coffee, the beans meet the scale. Weighing the grams of coffee used allows us to control one of the numerous variables in the complex formula of making coffee. However, if we change the amount of coffee beans used between extractions, we would also need to make corresponding adjustments to the other variables to compensate for this change.

Before we can act with precision, we must first understand the weight and intention of each decision. For this, we need an inner scale that is calibrated for the job. Introspection serves as that scale in life, helping us figure out which thoughts and desires carry real weight or importance and which are only passing impulses. Yet if our scale is miscalibrated, all measurements will be inaccurate, regardless of how careful or precise we are with our measurements. In other words, precision is not about perfection but about mindful attention to the small, often overlooked details that shape everything that follows. To calibrate and find balance through introspection requires us to pause in order to reset expectations, silence the noise, and focus on what truly matters. When we measure our effort, set strong intentions, and tend to the subtle choices, we create the balance that gives life its clarity.

Brew On These:
- What inner clarity are you missing before your actions can have the power and sharpness needed to change your life?
- Do you know what you want to do (and why) before you start anything, or do you just go with the flow and hope for the best?

PREPARING FOR CHAOS BEFORE SUCCESS

The difference between chaos and order is understanding. When we understand the cause of the chaos, we learn that even a small act done with understanding, rather than force, can restore order.

Grinding coffee beans without proper preparation can result in a mess. When coffee beans enter the grinder, the friction between the beans and the burrs of the grinder causes static electricity to build up. As a result, some of the coffee grounds exit the grinder unguided and stick to the grinder's surfaces instead of flowing straight into the basket of the portafilter. What should be a neat and focused process turns into chaos. But to reduce this chaos, the *Ross Droplet Technique* (RDT) recommends spraying the coffee beans with a small amount of water before grinding. This spritz of water helps tame the static electricity, allowing the coffee grounds to exit the grinder in a more orderly manner.

The energy that disrupts the grinding process is like the chaos within us that clouds our judgment and misguides our actions. We often rush into things without planning or aligning our thoughts and actions, which scatters our attention and efforts. To quell the chaos within us, we need to calm the mind first, much like how we calm the coffee beans with a spritz of water before grinding them. In our case, a small but mindful action, like taking a deep breath, setting a firm boundary, or visualizing our goal with clarity and purpose, can be the difference between unfocused effort and precise execution. The act of spritzing coffee beans is a reminder that there is always a way to find peace and balance, even when things are chaotic. Making the effort to prepare before we start can help us avoid making a mess in life.

Brew On These:
- What chaos in your life could be tempered with a small, intentional act? Could the chaos you are experiencing be genuine disorder, or might it stem from missed preparation or a gap in understanding?

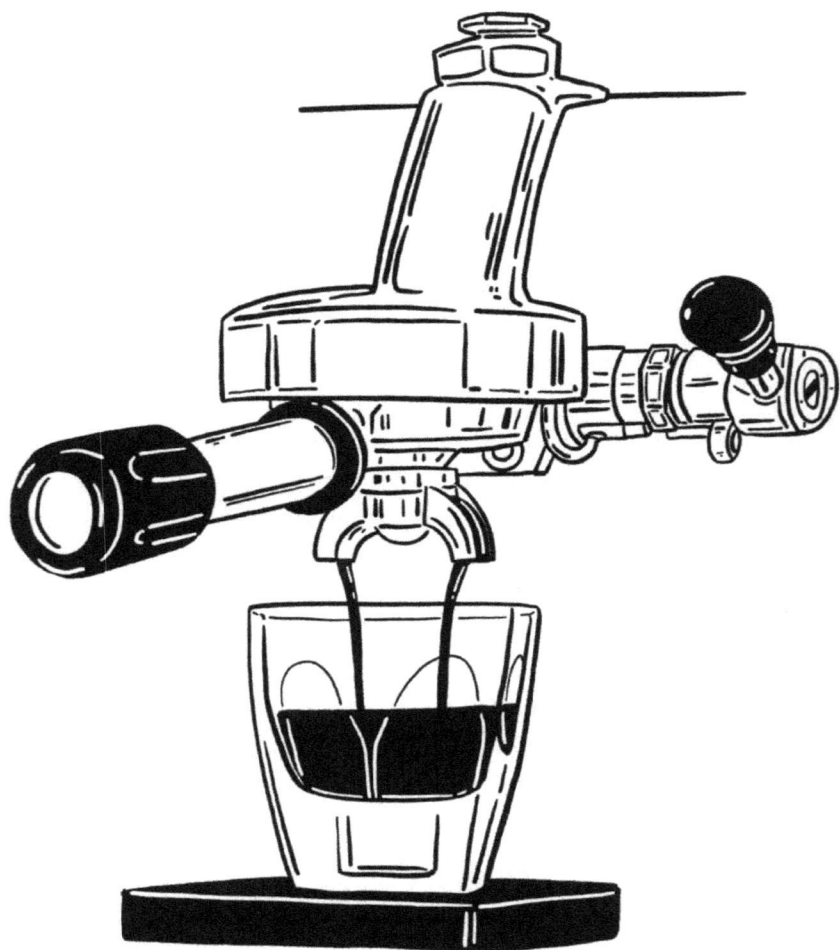

DIALING IN ON LIFE

The path to success may not be perfect on the first try. But through careful and intentional adjustments, we can refine the path and extract success.

When we grind whole beans, we risk grinding them too coarse or too fine, even if we use the same bag of coffee beans and the same grind setting as we did the day prior. What worked before may not always translate to today's success. To extract the best version of coffee, we need to know how to control and adjust the variables that affect the extraction, such as the weight of coffee beans used (the "*dose*"), the grind setting, the amount of coffee extracted (the "*yield*"), the temperature of water, and the amount of pressure applied during the extraction. Yet, before we can adjust any of these variables, we first need to carefully observe the extraction to understand what is off. These observations allow us to apply calibrated wisdom to determine which variable needs to be adjusted. This process of fine-tuning the variables in between extractions is referred to as "*dialing in.*"

We also need to "dial in" life every day to live well and be successful. What worked yesterday may not work today or tomorrow. Success does not always result from enormous leaps. Most often, we extract it through an iterative process of small, deliberate adjustments that demand patience, methodical refinement, and honest self-examination, much like a barista slowly adjusts a variable in between extractions until the desired extraction and results are achieved. To dial in life is to recognize that subtle, intentional changes in our habits, choices, and perspectives can create significant shifts in our trajectory. Over time, these measured adjustments compound, turning what once seemed unattainable into a consistent result of our efforts.

Brew On These:
- How often do you stop to reassess and recalibrate your approach, rather than accepting the outcome of your first attempt?
- What small adjustments could you make today that would help you face your challenges with greater precision and confidence?

SUCCESS DEMANDS ALIGNMENT

If our emotions and state of mind are uneven, no amount of effort will yield clarity or success. To extract success, order and balance must be achieved first.

To prepare the coffee grounds for extraction, the *Weiss Distribution Technique* (WDT) suggests gently stirring the coffee grounds in the portafilter with fine needles to break up clumps and distribute them evenly. Then, the coffee can be pressed into a unified bed or "*puck*" using a tamper (this step is referred to as "*tamping*"). But you need to use the correct amount of pressure to tamp the coffee grounds so that the puck has a consistent resistance, allowing the water to permeate evenly across and through the puck. If you skip these steps of declumping, distributing, and tamping the coffee grounds, the water will seek the path of least resistance during extraction and flow unevenly, like a river cutting through soft soil, leaving some parts of the coffee grounds untouched and other parts over-extracted. This uneven flow, referred to as "*channeling*," results in an espresso that fails to reflect the full flavors of the coffee.

The channeling that occurs during extraction serves as a reminder that, in life, the path of least resistance rarely leads to success. If we spread our energy too thin, group our efforts unevenly, or skip necessary steps in the process, we risk creating paths of least resistance where opportunities rush past us. To avoid channeling in life, we need to identify where we have let channels divert our energy and where resistance has become too strong, and then redistribute our energy and attention with care and intention. By doing this, we direct our efforts more evenly and give ourselves the best chance to achieve meaningful results.

Brew On These:
- What unseen clumps of thoughts may be getting in the way of your focus and making it harder to view things clearly?
- What small act can you do today to bring you more balance?

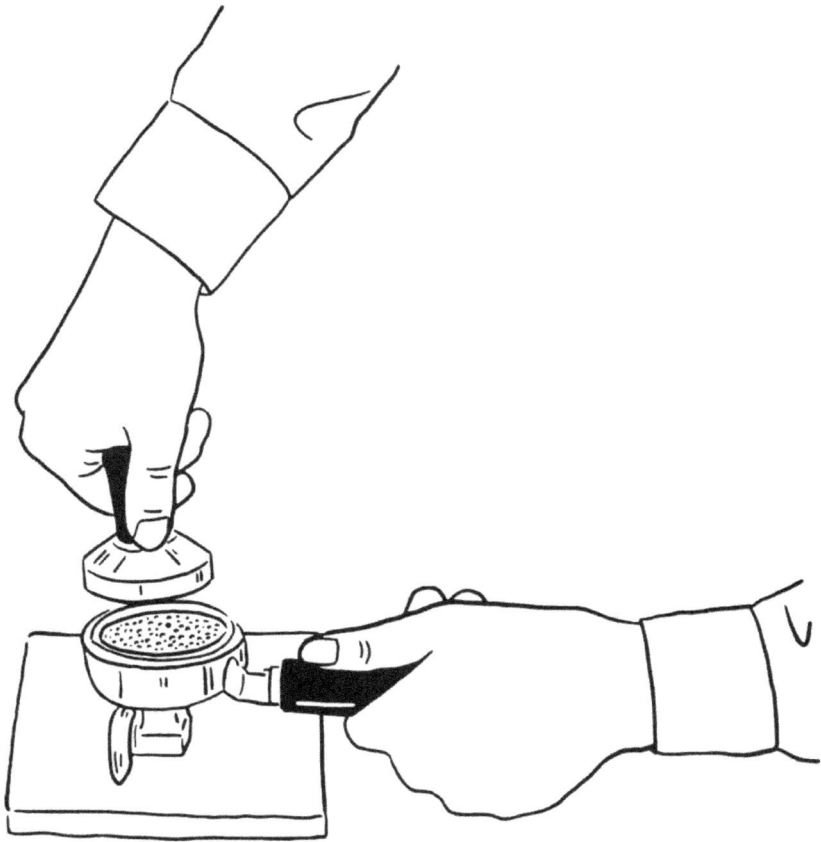

RINSING THE FILTER

*A clouded mind allows the impurities to seep into every choice, tainting even
your best efforts. To lay the foundation for success, clear away the impurities
that cloud your judgment and vision.*

In a world of expensive machines and complex equipment, the
pour-over stands out as a simple and manual way to make coffee,
requiring only a cone-shaped dripper, a paper filter, a mug, hot water,
and, of course, ground coffee. But before you start a pour-over, you
need to rinse the paper filter. The paper filter may appear clean and
white, but it may contain unnoticeable impurities, such as small amounts
of paper fibers, processing chemicals, and residual materials from the
production process. If you don't properly rinse the filter, these
impurities will seep through the filter while brewing and ruin the taste
and quality of the coffee.

Rinsing the filter is a reminder that preparation begins with
removing things that interfere with our success. Just as an unrinsed filter
cannot produce a clean cup, an unprepared mind cannot produce clarity
or direction. In life, the residue is not paper fibers but the distractions,
impulses, and biases that cling to the mind. If we rush ahead without
rinsing them away, everything that flows through us, such as our feelings
and emotions, will be tainted by the residues. Each day presents us with
the opportunity to release what no longer serves us and prepare
ourselves for what truly matters. Only then can what flows through us
be balanced, intentional, and pure.

Brew On These:
- What distractions or habits are currently clouding your mind and
  actions?
- How can you make it a daily practice to clear your mind? What
  small act, like journaling, meditation, or a simple pause, could help
  you think and act with greater clarity?

THE BALANCING ACT

Just like minerals balance water to make the perfect espresso, virtues must balance the soul for us to fulfill our purpose.

Water is life, and it's the soul of coffee. The same minerals in water that are essential for our bodies to function also play an important role in awakening the spirit of coffee. But not all water is the same. Our drinking water contains minerals, such as calcium, magnesium, sodium, sulfate, and potassium. The proportion of these minerals in water depends on the source of the water, which is why water can taste different depending on its origin. When brewing coffee, excessive amounts of any one mineral can alter the taste of the extracted coffee. Calcium strengthens the body and feel of the coffee, but too much calcium changes the texture. Magnesium enhances the coffee's notes, including acidity, floral, fruity, sweet, and chocolate notes. But if the water has too much magnesium, the coffee will taste bitter. To manage the mineral balance in water used for coffee, some companies sell mineral tablets or powders that can be added to distilled water to produce a water profile specifically designed to enhance the coffee's flavors.

Virtues shape the soul in the same way minerals shape water: they give it life, character, and depth. But just like the minerals in water, the balance of our virtues matters. When we lack sufficient virtue, life drifts aimlessly, and excessive virtue can overwhelm our character and misguide our actions. Practical wisdom is what keeps virtues in balance, allowing them to work together and help us become better individuals. Just as balanced water reveals the true nature of coffee, a soul balanced by virtues reveals our true nature.

Brew On These:
- Do you have the right mix of virtues in your life (power, courage, balance, etc.) to bring out the best in you?
- What virtues do you need to strengthen or develop in order to align with who you want to be?

TEND WHAT TENDS YOU

Our main tools for success are our bodies and minds. But if we neglect them, they will fail us when we need them most. An essential part of preparing for success is maintaining these tools with care for those moments when their performance becomes indispensable.

Regularly cleaning our coffee equipment is not just good practice but also an essential element in sustaining success. When we neglect our tools, we allow hidden buildup to ruin their quality and performance. For instance, the mineral deposit scale that builds up in a coffee machine's boiler can cause erratic pressure drops and temperature fluctuations. As a result, our machines become less effective and more prone to chronic issues, similar to how chronic stress builds up over time, making us less clear-headed and less able to perform. In the same way, residual oils from coffee grounds can build up over time in the grinder, brew basket, and portafilter. As these oils build up, they become rancid and spoil our brew, just as neglected emotions linger beneath the surface, quietly tainting how we think, feel, and act. Likewise, a neglected grinder still works, but it produces coffee grounds that are inconsistent, resulting in extractions that are equally inconsistent, much like how the gradual buildup of fatigue and mental clutter can clog and slow down our internal systems and diminish our performance.

Every time we clean our tools is an intentional reset and a testament to the value of steady and mindful care. The inner work we do today helps us succeed tomorrow. Just as a descaling solution breaks down the buildup of scale in a boiler, frequent self-care and self-reflection dissolve the unseen accumulation of mental residue, allowing us to be at our best for those moments that matter most.

Brew On These:
- What parts of your life operate daily but suffer from neglect? When was the last time you took a moment to address any internal buildup (emotions, outdated assumptions, anxieties, etc.)?

This page is an intentional pause . . .

breathe in calm . . . breathe out stress.

PART III

From Bean to Being — Brewing a Life of Success & Meaning

TRUE WORTH BEYOND PRICE

Do not chase the praise of others, for it rises today and sets tomorrow.
Instead, anchor yourself to the work that sustains and fulfills you.

Before we can brew a life of meaning and success, we need to consider what is truly worth valuing. Coffee is traded as a commodity, like sugar and cotton. The price of coffee fluctuates based on factors that affect supply and demand, such as weather, politics, and growing consumer demand. In particular, climate change threatens the delicate areas where coffee grows best today, increasing the risk that these lands may not be viable tomorrow. Although we can't control all of these factors, we can choose the price we are willing to pay. So, while external forces dictate the market price, the value we assign to coffee is determined by what the coffee means to us and what it provides us, like warmth and comfort in the morning rush and focus when our thoughts and attention are scattered.

Success in life is often viewed as a commodity, measured by the standards of value that the world sets, such as titles, wealth, and influence. However, true success is not defined by the changing opinions of others. Like a cup brewed for your taste, we each have a different definition of success, and we can assign a different value to the same thing. When we anchor our definition of success with what nourishes the soul, we rise above the shifting standards of society. By doing so, we free ourselves to pursue what sustains us, aligns us with our purpose, and endures through life's changing seasons. This type of freedom cannot be quantified.

Brew On These:
- If the definition of success shifts with the winds, how do you anchor your measurement of success and meaning?
- What aspects of your growth matter to you and continue to shape you, even when the world doesn't value them?

RITUALS SHAPE SUCCESS

A life well-brewed is not the result of a single morning, but of countless mornings tended with intention and care.

A ritual is a series of actions performed in a specific order on a regular basis. Our coffee routine is a form of a ritual that anchors our mornings. We usually perform each step in a specific order: weighing the beans, grinding them, extracting the espresso, and then enjoying our coffee. But even if we follow and execute our routine perfectly, it does not guarantee a flawless extraction or a perfect espresso. Rituals do not guarantee a specific outcome. Instead, rituals channel chaos into order and guide our attention to the present moment. Our coffee ritual helps us better understand the complexities of the brewing process and sharpens our mastery and control over the variables that affect the process.

Each repetition of this ritual becomes a type of meditation. The countless mornings we spend honoring this ritual teach us how to read the language of extraction, understand the intimate relationship between the coffee grounds and the water, and grasp the subtle interactions between time and temperature. These lessons sharpen our perception of each variable in the brewing equation and the final product. Through this ritual, we evolve from merely following instructions to mastering the craft. So, even though our ritual will not guarantee an outcome, it creates and arranges the conditions that make success more likely, just like a gardener prepares the soil and takes care of the plant, even though they can't make it grow fruit.

Brew On These:
- In what parts of your life do you have to do the same thing over and over? How can being present and mindful during this routine transform it into something profound and lasting?

WHEN TO ACT

To determine when to act, listen to your body and mind rather than the tick-tock of the clock. Let readiness, not routine, guide you.

Is there a perfect time to drink coffee? How long should we wait after we get up to have our first cup? How close to bedtime can we drink a cup without ruining our sleep? Overall, it's not when you drink coffee that matters most, but how you listen to your body when it calls for coffee and how mindful you are when you do so. Every day is unique, and yesterday's routine may be out of sync with the rhythm of today. Some mornings call for coffee right after we wake up, while others tell us to wait until later.

Although there are numerous benefits of following a routine, we should only act when we are ready. To determine if you are ready, pause to listen to your body and mind, not just to figure out what to do, but also to understand what they want. During this pause, we learn to become aware of ourselves and the signs that indicate to us that we are ready for action. Learning to drink coffee only when we are genuinely ready and aware becomes a practice in honoring timing. In life, like in coffee, being ready makes a difference. A rushed decision, like a quickly made cup of coffee, can leave a bitter taste that lasts long after the moment has passed. But when we wait with purpose and act with intention, we give ideas and opportunities time to ripen into their full potential. Through this approach, we learn that success doesn't depend on how fast we move but on how ready we are when we choose to act.

Brew On These:
- In what moments have you rushed forward, acting from urgency, believing you were ready? Did the urgency come from within or from external pressures?
- How do you know when it's time to act? What signs in your body or your mind tell you that you are ready and that the moment is right?

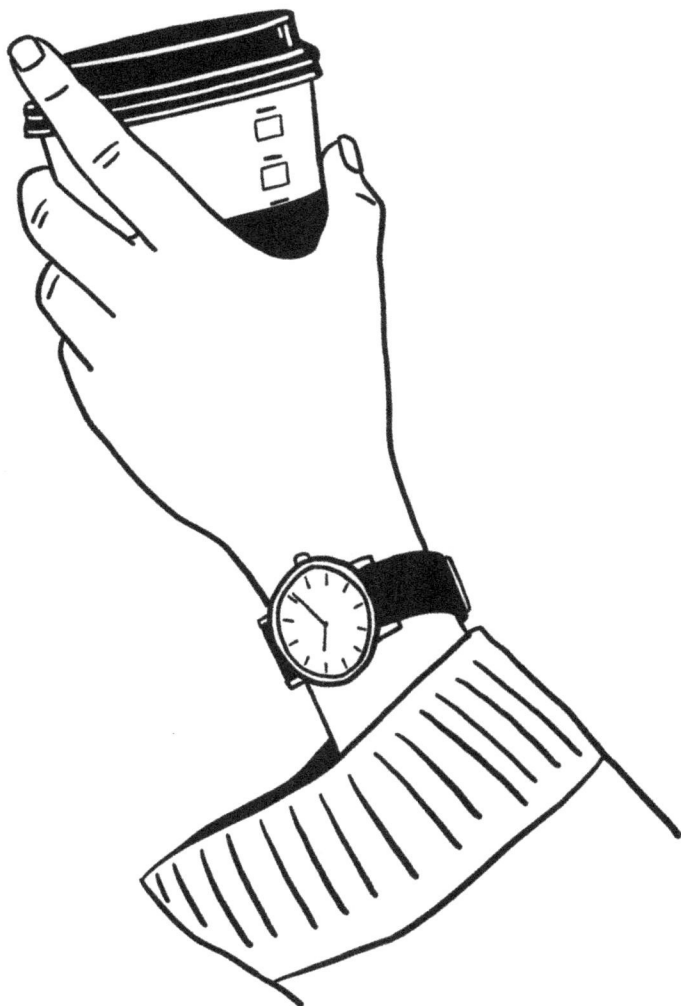

THE BARISTA'S DANCE

No matter the circumstances or constraints, move with purpose and measured grace. Life is a dance.

In the busy morning rush, baristas move with a precise choreography born of necessity and practice in the small areas behind the counter that make up their stage. Every movement has a purpose and flows with the next one. Each barista knows their role, place, and rhythm. They develop the discipline to act at the right time and the patience to wait when necessary, moving in harmony with their peers and the world around them.

Life often resembles these crowded spaces behind the counters, and how we learn to move with purpose within the limits of life determines the extent to which we can achieve our goals. We won't always have the best conditions or all the resources to thrive. But to succeed in life, we need to learn how to perform even when things are difficult. While not an ideal situation, having limited tools or resources pushes us to be more creative, just like the barista who adapts their measured choreography to the constrained layout of their work environment. These limitations make us focus on what is important, eliminate any unnecessary energy, and move with purpose. By embracing this framework, we can learn to act with greater intention and purpose. Over time, you will move and flow with a natural grace, like a practiced dance in harmony with the rhythms of life.

Brew On These:
- How do you choose to move in life? Do you listen to the underlying rhythm of your surroundings and act to this beat? Or do you move to a beat entirely your own?
- What challenges or constraints in your life have helped you dance towards a meaningful life instead of getting in the way?

GUIDING THE FLOW OF TRANSFORMATION

The finest outcomes in life come from being ready before you take action and sustaining your momentum once in motion.

Making coffee is a delicate art that requires care and control. To start pulling an espresso, a small amount of water is slowly introduced to soak the coffee grounds just enough to let them bloom. The goal of this first step in the transformation process, called "*preinfusion*," is not to extract coffee but to wake up the coffee grounds and prepare them for the next stage. Without preinfusion, the coffee grounds wouldn't be ready to withstand the full flow of water, and the water would rush through the grounds unevenly, leaving some parts untouched and others too wet. This uneven flow of water results in an unbalanced extraction. Just as the preinfusion stage lays the foundation for a great brew, taking time to work through our goals with care and preparation sets the foundation for balanced and satisfying results in life.

After preinfusion, the water flow is gradually increased to extract the coffee's full potential. In this act of measured control, referred to as "*flow control*," the water flow is carefully managed to guide the extraction towards balance and harmony. The goal is to maintain a constant flow that draws out the depth and richness of the coffee, but not so quickly that the water rushes through unchanged. Ultimately, flow control is the discipline of momentum. In life, momentum needs to be sustained and guided towards our purpose. That is why learning to adjust the speed of our actions to match the harmony of our goals is the key to getting the most out of ourselves and extracting a life of success.

Brew On These:
- Are you just going with the flow and letting it take you where it wants? If you need to guide momentum with intention, how would you plan each act before and after the flow starts?

THE POWER OF PRESSURE

Just as the right pressure brings forth the full flavor of espresso, we must also apply force in life with balance to reveal strength and clarity.

Pressure is an important variable in making coffee, and the right amount of pressure is critical for extracting the coffee's spirit. If you don't use enough pressure during extraction, the coffee will taste weak and sour. This kind of result is known as *"under-extraction."* But if you apply too much pressure, the coffee will taste bitter. This kind of result is called *"over-extraction."* The amount of pressure that is applied depends on what we are trying to achieve. There is a reason why advanced coffee machines have multiple pressure gauges to measure the pressure level in different parts of the machine. For instance, one gauge is used to monitor the pressure in the portafilter group head, which is where the water meets the coffee grounds, and another gauge is used to monitor the pressure for the steam wand used to heat up and texturize milk.

Just as the right amount of pressure during extraction unlocks the richness and essence of coffee, learning to balance pressure in our lives helps unlock our deepest potential. Without challenges in life, we remain untested and underdeveloped. But when controlled correctly, pressure pushes us to our limits and awakens qualities within us that we might not have known we possessed, just as a blacksmith uses heat and force to transform soft metals into a stronger version. In this way, pressure clarifies who we are and reveals the strength of character that comfort alone cannot produce. So don't avoid pressure altogether, but constantly monitor the amount of pressure you face and adjust as needed.

Brew On These:
- What parts of your life are you putting too much pressure on, and what parts are you pushing back against in a way that stops you from growing?
- How can you better deal with and control stress in your life to help you reach your full potential?

FAITH IN THE FLAWED

Learn to care deeply and give your full effort, but also learn to meet the outcome with presence. This is the grace that turns imperfection into wisdom.

Even the most disciplined brewing process, executed with precision, cannot guarantee that every cup will be flawless. There are times when we are steaming milk that just won't texture right, no matter how carefully we pay attention to the temperature and method. The result is milk foam that is either too thin or too stiff to make latte art. On other mornings, the espresso might extract a little too quickly, or the water temperature might fluctuate just enough to change the extraction. And yet, even when our equipment falters or our skills fall short, the coffee still offers us comfort, warmth, and a sense of purpose. The meditative practice, then, is to learn how to receive each imperfect cup with grace.

The complexity and unpredictability of life remind us that outcomes often defy our best intentions, regardless of how pure or precise our efforts may be. A cup can fall short in form (like under-aerated milk that may not support latte art) and still succeed in function (like taste and comfort), just as a life can be deeply meaningful even when it does not unfold exactly as we planned. But this perspective is not a call to abandon our pursuits of precision and care. On the contrary, this commitment to act with precision sharpens our awareness and allows us to accept whatever may unfold from the process, whether flawless or flawed. And when we learn to accept those imperfections, we discover that success and meaning are not measured by how the results of our efforts look to us or to others but by how profoundly those efforts serve our purpose and transform the way we live.

Brew On These:
- In what ways do you rush past imperfect outcomes instead of sitting with them long enough to discover the lessons they carry?
- What shift or adjustment could help you continue to strive for excellence without attaching your worth to every result? How could this shift affect your effort and growth?

BALANCING THE BREW FOR YOU

Live in a way that is true to you, knowing that your life is yours to shape.
Only you can decide what fulfills you and gives your days meaning.

Choosing whether or not to add sugar to your coffee is a quiet act of intentionally living in which the choice reflects your true intention. Some people like their coffee black because they enjoy its raw and pure flavors. Others add sugar to soften the coffee's bitterness and make it easier to drink. Just like how one person's cup of coffee might be too strong or too sweet for someone else, we all have different levels of tolerance for life's struggles and bitterness. Life, like coffee, makes us choose how we face what is difficult. Sometimes it's best to face difficulties head-on. At other times, it's best to soften the sharpness so we can keep moving forward in a way that better suits our purpose. Neither approach is wrong. The key is to remember that the cup we make and the life we live are both unique to us, and living with intention means owning those choices. If we surrender our choices to the opinions of others, we lose the freedom to shape a life that is truly our own.

Nonetheless, changing how we face the bitterness of life is not avoiding the truth. Instead, it offers us a way to engage with the bitterness in a new light, much like sugar transforms coffee into something more approachable for those who otherwise avoid it without sugar. What may satisfy or comfort one person may leave another unfulfilled or unmoved, so how we choose to balance our cup or life is a deeply personal act of intentional living.

Brew On These:
- Are there parts of your life you accept exactly as they unfold without asking whether they still serve your purpose?
- Have you given yourself the peace to shape your life the way you want it to be, even if others doubt how you're doing it?

PLACE AS PURPOSE

Your thoughts and experiences are shaped by the places where you choose to be, so intentionally choose spaces that reflect the order and clarity you seek.

The quality of the beans and the precision of the extraction process are not the only things that enhance our experience with coffee. Where we consume our coffee also directly impacts our experience with it. A coffee shop illustrates this truth. The orchestra of noises, the soft hum of conversations, and the steady streams of strangers all contribute to the ambiance. Above it all, the melodies from carefully curated playlists seem to be in sync with the vibrations of our souls and the broader pulse of the universe. This could explain why some coffee shops speak to your soul, while others may not. Even drinking coffee next to a sunlit window can make us experience it differently than when we drink it next to the same window on a gray, rainy day. Although the beans and brewing process remain unchanged, the brightness of sunshine or the peaceful falling rain affect how we feel and what we experience.

Choosing a space with care anchors us in how we want to live. A setting that radiates calm and order mirrors the peace we seek in life. A well-organized environment, like a well-ordered mind, makes it easier to focus intensely, let go of distractions, and allow the mind to settle. In such a place, even the simple act of drinking coffee naturally evolves into a mindful practice. In the end, the space you choose matters. Whether it's a coffee shop that speaks to you, a sunlit corner at home, or any space where you feel at ease, choosing your space intentionally roots you in purpose and aligns you with order and harmony.

Brew On These:

- What do the places you choose to be in say about the standards you have for your own growth and success?
- Where in your life have you felt most alive, focused, or at peace? Are there any similarities between these places?

THE FINAL SIP

Remember, all pleasures are temporary. Cherish them while they last, and accept that every moment, like every cup of coffee, will come to an end.

A full cup of coffee is a rush of pleasure for the senses: the rich aroma that rises, the comforting warmth radiating through the hands that cradle the cup, and the first sip that wakes up our taste buds with promise. It is a moment of abundance when every sense is engaged and brimming with anticipation of the next sip. We pour our time, care, and energy into making a cup of coffee. Yet, as we progress from a full cup to an empty cup, the last drop often escapes our attention. Does its place at the end make it less worthy? Does our awareness fade away along with the transient warmth of the coffee? The first sip is easy to celebrate, while the sips in the middle comfort us. But the last sip, cooled down from its earlier heat, is different from all prior sips and carries the concentrated essence of everything that came before it. This last sip invites us to slow down and recognize that the end does not take away from the beginning.

In life, we also celebrate and remember our firsts, but we often rush past the quiet endings that hold their own meaning, distracted by the next thing that catches our attention. As this final chapter closes, may it remind us that a meaningful life is not defined only by beginnings or peak moments. Brewing a meaningful life requires us to move through every stage of our journey with intention and purpose, until who we are and how we live become the true measure of success. This is both the challenge and the invitation. To brew your life as you would a cup of coffee: choosing your conditions with care, embracing the process with patience, and trusting that richness comes from honoring every stage. In the end, brew your life your way and savor every moment of it.

Brew On These:
- When the cup is almost empty, how do you honor what remains? Do you rush to finish or pause to enjoy what you have left?
- Which lessons in this book have resonated with you the most?

This page is an intentional pause . . .

let this moment settle.

THE PRACTICE

The following tables compile the meditations into a framework for living. Use these tables to review, reflect, and practice at your own pace.

Part I: The Growth & Transformation Cycle	
Chapter	**Meditation**
The Right Environment	*Be mindful of the environments where you choose to grow.*
Cultivating Patience	*To be patient does not imply doing nothing. Being patient means being in harmony with nature and trusting the process without demanding an immediate reward.*
Precision Over Speed	*It is not the quantity of experiences that shapes you most deeply, but the care with which you approach those moments. How you harvest life's moments reflects what you value most.*
Sorting And Letting Go With Purpose	*Not everything that grows with you is meant to continue with you. Part of growth is learning to release what no longer serves you so you can carry forward only what aligns with your values and purpose.*
Methods of Maturation	*It is not just that we endure, but how we endure that determines the depth of who we become.*
Unconventional Methods, Profound Results	*Do not fear the unfamiliar path. Growth often requires us to reject old methods that no longer serve us.*
From Raw To Ready	*Avoiding challenges means remaining raw, undeveloped, and untested. The heat of the challenges we fear is often what we need to reveal our essence.*
Transformation Requires Integration	*To be transformed means not just to change but also to absorb the change. After any transformation, take a moment to pause and align yourself with the changes you experienced.*
Unified, Not Uniform	*Character is not born from uniformity, but from the careful blending of opposing elements into something richer than their parts.*
Life's Daily Grind	*Change doesn't always arrive gently. Sometimes change destroys what we thought was permanent, not to punish us, but to prepare us for a deeper purpose.*

Part II: Preparing for Success & The Tools to Achieve It	
Chapter	**Meditation**
Respect The Hidden Order of Success	*No matter how small the task, the quality of the outcome is determined by the care and mindfulness with which we approach it.*
Tools For Success	*True readiness is less about the number of tools you have and more about having the wisdom to choose and apply them right. Even the right tool that is misapplied becomes the wrong choice.*
The Right Vessel	*Not every cup is made to hold every brew. Preparing for success starts with choosing what fits not just in form but also in purpose. What looks right at first may not necessarily serve who you are becoming.*
The Weight of Precision	*Before action, weigh. Before weighing, pause and reset. Before resetting, begin with clarity of intent.*
Preparing For Chaos Before Success	*The difference between chaos and order is understanding. When we understand the cause of the chaos, we learn that even a small act done with understanding, rather than force, can restore order.*
Dialing In On Life	*The path to success may not be perfect on the first try. But through careful and intentional adjustments, we can refine the path and extract success.*
Success Demands Alignment	*If our emotions and state of mind are uneven, no amount of effort will yield clarity or success. To extract success, order and balance must be achieved first.*
Rinsing The Filter	*A clouded mind allows the impurities to seep into every choice, tainting even your best efforts. To lay the foundation for success, clear away the impurities that cloud your judgment and vision.*
The Balancing Act	*Just like minerals balance water to make the perfect espresso, virtues must balance the soul for us to fulfill our purpose.*
Tend What Tends You	*Our main tools for success are our bodies and minds. But if we neglect them, they will fail us when we need them most. An essential part of preparing for success is maintaining these tools with care for those moments when their performance becomes indispensable.*

Part III: From Bean to Being – Brewing a Life of Success & Meaning	
Chapter	**Meditation**
True Worth Beyond Price	*Do not chase the praise of others, for it rises today and sets tomorrow. Instead, anchor yourself to the work that sustains and fulfills you.*
Rituals Shape Success	*A life well-brewed is not the result of a single morning, but of countless mornings tended with intention and care.*
When To Act	*To determine when to act, listen to your body and mind rather than the tick-tock of the clock. Let readiness, not routine, guide you.*
The Barista's Dance	*No matter the circumstances or constraints, move with purpose and measured grace. Life is a dance.*
Guiding The Flow of Transformation	*The finest outcomes in life come from being ready before you take action and sustaining your momentum once in motion.*
The Power of Pressure	*Just as the right pressure brings forth the full flavor of espresso, we must also apply force in life with balance to reveal strength and clarity.*
Faith In The Flawed	*Learn to care deeply and give your full effort, but also learn to meet the outcome with presence. This is the grace that turns imperfection into wisdom.*
Balancing The Brew For You	*Live in a way that is true to you, knowing that your life is yours to shape. Only you can decide what fulfills you and gives your days meaning.*
Place As Purpose	*Your thoughts and experiences are shaped by the places where you choose to be, so intentionally choose spaces that reflect the order and clarity you seek.*
The Last Sip	*Remember, all pleasures are temporary. Cherish them while they last, and accept that every moment, like every cup of coffee, will come to an end.*

BEHIND THE BREW

In this section, I would like to provide you with a brief glimpse into the process of *creating* this book, including the writing, thinking, designing, curating, and learning that went into each part. By taking the time and space to honor this process, I hope it will give you a deeper appreciation for the book.

Creating Through Burnout

As mentioned in the Introduction, this book began as a personal project to help me process and clarify what I was learning about coffee and life. Along the way, *creating* this book became a path to reclaiming my thoughts and creative energy, both of which had been overshadowed by burnout. In the early stages of this process, I struggled to stay motivated and lacked clarity about what I wanted to do. I felt distant from the creative outlets I used to enjoy before experiencing burnout. But as I committed to this project, I began showing up for myself again. The process pushed me to be more consistent, to listen closely to when I needed to pause, and to approach the work with patience. In doing so, I slowly reconnected with my sense of focus, creativity, and presence.

Structure With Intention

In the Introduction, I only previewed that each chapter, or essay, was precisely one single page in length. But I did not explain why I decided to take this approach. In short, I wanted every idea to be fully contained on a single page, as a way to hold my attention while drafting and yours while reading, without the distraction of turning pages. While reading and writing, our momentum and focus are often disrupted when a thought spans multiple pages. By keeping the meditations, reflections, and questions all in view on the same page, each chapter becomes complete in itself, and nothing is left behind or forgotten. This structure also quiets the subtle impatience we feel when we don't know where a chapter will end, allowing us to settle in, concentrate, and engage more deeply with the content immediately in front of us.

However, this one-page format imposed restrictions on the number of words I could fit into each chapter, requiring me to sharpen my writing and make each word count and each concept concise. Still, as I reread the manuscript while editing, I recognized that there may be gaps in my logic or in the connections I made between the coffee-related lessons and the broader lessons on life. Perhaps this may be due in part to my bias as the author, failing to see what you, as the reader, may miss or struggle to understand, even if it all makes sense to me. Yet even this serves as another reminder of the lessons on clarity shared throughout this book. What seems clear to me may not be so obvious to you. Part of the work towards a life of clarity is pausing to check our assumptions and steadily refining our thoughts and actions until they reflect what we truly seek.

Designing With Purpose

After completing the first draft of this book, I wanted to let the manuscript rest for a few days before beginning the editing process. In the meantime, I turned to thinking about the design concept for the front cover. Over the following week, I searched for the right idea to anchor the front cover design, but none captured what I felt was the essence of this book. Then, one night at around 3 a.m., I woke up with an idea in mind based on an image I had previously come across during my initial search. However, instead of using the entire image for the cover, I wanted to zoom in on a specific area, focusing on the moment when milk and coffee swirl together. That single moment serves as a reminder to be intentional about what we pour into ourselves, such as clarity, balance, depth, and patience.

In many ways, the process of designing the cover mirrored my process of writing the book (which I discussed in the Introduction to this book). Writing the book and designing the cover pushed me to think through the moments of inspiration and refine those ideas to reflect my vision. Through this process, I learned that the answer is already within me and that sometimes I just need to zoom in and look more closely.

Curating The Illustrations

While I didn't create the illustrations and images used in this book, I spent hours carefully curating them to ensure they aligned with each reflection both in tone and in rhythm. They also had to work well in black and white print, feel cohesive across the book (particularly in style since different artists made the illustrations[1]), and visually echo the reflections without overwhelming them. This part of the process reminded me of the lessons I discussed in this book's chapter, *"Sorting and Letting Go With Purpose."* Like sorting the coffee cherries and letting go of those that don't meet the standard, curating the illustrations for this book required me to stay true to the principle that what I leave out matters just as much as what I include.

Learning to Take Ownership

Creating this book meant learning, revising, starting over, and figuring things out along the way. Each design decision, each word, and each revision was a chance for me to trust myself more deeply and own my decisions (and my mistakes). Ultimately, the creative process and this book are about paying attention to your thoughts, taking control of your process, and trusting your ability to create something meaningful.

---

[1] Note, the illustrations reproduced in this book are used under license from Shutterstock.com.

FURTHER READING

Still brewing? Consider pouring into these books next:

1. *Meditations* by Marcus Aurelius
2. *The Daily Stoic* by Ryan Holiday & Stephen Hanselman
3. *Stillness Is the Key* by Ryan Holiday
4. *The Art of Simple Living* by Shunmyō Masuno
5. *Radical Acceptance* by Tara Brach
6. *Atomic Habits* by James Clear
7. *Zen and the Art of Motorcycle Maintenance* by Robert M. Pirsig
8. *Wabi Sabi: Japanese Wisdom for a Perfectly Imperfect Life* by Beth Kempton
9. *The War of Art* by Steven Pressfield
10. *How to Do Nothing* by Jenny Odell
11. *A Guide to the Good Life: The Ancient Art of Stoic Joy* by William B. Irvine
12. *In Praise of Shadows* by Jun'ichirō Tanizaki
13. *The Prophet* by Kahlil Gibran
14. *Artful Design: Technology in Search of the Sublime* by Ge Wang
15. *Manual for Living* by Epictetus (various translations)
16. *When Things Fall Apart* by Pema Chödrön
17. *Braiding Sweetgrass* by Robin Wall Kimmerer
18. *The Book of Delights* by Ross Gay

THE LANGUAGE OF COFFEE

The world of coffee has its own language, and some of the coffee-related terms and expressions can be difficult to understand without any prior knowledge. This brief glossary aims to define certain key words and terms, but note that it's not an exhaustive list.

Agtron Scale – A system for measuring the roast color of coffee beans.

Americano – Espresso mixed with hot water, similar in strength to regular drip coffee.

Arabica – A variety of coffee known for smooth, mild flavors. Most specialty coffee is Arabica.

Blend – Coffee made from mixing beans from different regions or varieties.

Bloom – The bubbles that form when hot water first hits fresh coffee grounds, releasing gas.

Body – The weight or thickness of coffee in your mouth, ranging from light to heavy.

Cappuccino – Espresso with steamed milk and a thick layer of milk foam on top.

Cascara – The dried husk of the coffee cherry.

Chaff – The thin, papery skin that comes off coffee beans during roasting.

Channeling – When water flows unevenly through an espresso puck, causing poor extraction.

Coffee Belt – The regions around the equator where coffee grows best, between the Tropics of Cancer and Capricorn.

Coffee Cherries – The fruit of the coffee plant, which contains the coffee beans (seeds).

Cold Brew – Coffee made by steeping grounds in cold water for several hours, resulting in a smooth, less acidic drink.

Crema – The golden foam on top of a freshly pulled espresso shot.

Cupping – A formal tasting method used to evaluate coffee's aroma and flavor.

De-gassing – The process of roasted coffee beans releasing trapped gases, such as carbon dioxide, after roasting.

Decaf – Coffee with most of the caffeine removed.

Density – How heavy or compact coffee beans are, often linked to quality.

Dialing In – The process of adjusting grind, dose, and brewing time to get the best-tasting espresso.

Direct Trade – When coffee roasters purchase beans directly from farmers, rather than through intermediaries.

Doppio – A double shot of espresso.

Dose – The amount of ground coffee used for brewing.

Drip Coffee – Coffee brewed by letting hot water drip through grounds in a filter (typical home coffee maker).

Espresso – Strong, concentrated coffee brewed by forcing hot water through finely ground beans.

Extraction – The process of pulling flavors out of coffee grounds with water.

Filter Coffee – Any coffee brewed through a filter, such as drip or pour-over.

First Crack – The popping sound beans make during roasting when they expand and release gases.

Flat White – Similar to a latte, but with less milk and a thinner layer of foam.

Floaters – Unripe or defective coffee cherries that float to the top during sorting.

Flow Control – The ability to control the speed and pressure of water when brewing espresso.

French Press – A brewing method where coffee grounds steep in hot water, then are separated with a plunger.

Green Coffee – Raw, unroasted coffee beans.

Green Grading – The sorting of unroasted coffee beans by size, shape, and quality.

Grind Size – How fine or coarse coffee beans are ground, which affects how they brew.

Honey Process – A coffee processing method where some of the sticky fruit (mucilage) is left on the bean during drying, creating sweet flavors.

Knock Box – A container used to knock out and collect used espresso pucks.

Latte – Espresso with steamed milk and a small layer of foam, creamy and mild.

Latte Art – Designs made in a coffee's milk foam, often by skilled baristas.

Lungo – A "long shot" of espresso, made with more water, producing a diluted espresso.

Macchiato – Espresso with just a small "mark" of milk foam on top.

Microfoam – Very fine, smooth milk foam used in lattes and cappuccinos.

Mocha – A latte with chocolate added.

Mucilage – The sticky, sugary layer surrounding the coffee bean inside the cherry.

Natural Process – A way of drying coffee beans inside the fruit, creating fruity flavors.

Origin – The country or region where coffee is grown, influencing its flavor profile.

Over-extraction – When coffee is brewed for too long, using water that is too hot, or with too fine a grind, resulting in bitter flavors.

Parchment – The thin, papery layer that remains around coffee beans after the fruit has been removed.

Peaberry – A rare coffee bean where only one seed grows inside the coffee fruit instead of two.

Portafilter – The handle and basket that holds coffee grounds in an espresso machine.

Pour-Over – Brewing method where hot water is poured by hand over coffee grounds in a filter.

Preinfusion – The first stage of brewing espresso, where a small amount of water wets the puck before full pressure.

Puck – The compacted coffee grounds left after brewing espresso.

Ristretto – A "short shot" of espresso, more concentrated and intense.

Roast – The process of heating green coffee beans until they turn brown and develop flavor.

Robusta – A variety of coffee known for its strong, bold flavor and higher caffeine content than Arabica coffee.

Ross Droplet Technique (RDT) – Spraying beans lightly with water before grinding to reduce static and clumping.

Second Crack – The second round of popping sounds in roasting, marking darker roasts.

Silverskin – A thin layer of skin that clings to beans, sometimes flaking off after roasting.

Single Origin – Coffee beans that all come from one specific region or farm.

Specialty Coffee – High-quality coffee graded 80 points or above on a 100-point scale.

Tamping – Pressing ground coffee evenly into the portafilter before brewing espresso.

Under-extraction – When coffee is brewed too quickly or with too coarse a grind, resulting in sour or weak flavors.

Weiss Distribution Technique (WDT) – A method of stirring espresso grounds with fine needles to distribute evenly before tamping.

Washed Process – Removing the outer and inner layers of the coffee cherries, leaving only the coffee beans to be dried.

Water Activity – A measure of water in green coffee that affects shelf life and quality.

Yield – The final amount of brewed coffee compared to the dose of grounds used.

BIBLIOGRAPHY

1. Davids, Kenneth. *Coffee: A Guide to Buying, Brewing, and Enjoying.* 7th ed. New York: St. Martin's Griffin, 2018.

2. Hoffmann, James. T*he World Atlas of Coffee: From Beans to Brewing – Coffees Explored, Explained and Enjoyed.* 2nd ed. London: Octopus Publishing Group, 2018.

3. Illy, Ernesto, and Rinantonio Viani, eds. *Espresso Coffee: The Science of Quality.* 2nd ed. London: Elsevier Academic Press, 2005.

4. International Coffee Organization (ICO). *Glossary and Coffee Market Reports.* London: ICO. http://www.ico.org.

5. Lingle, Ted R. *The Coffee Cupper's Handbook: Systematic Guide to the Sensory Evaluation of Coffee's Flavor.* 3rd ed. Long Beach, CA: Specialty Coffee Association of America, 2011.

6. Pendergrast, Mark. *Uncommon Grounds: The History of Coffee and How It Transformed Our World.* Revised ed. New York: Basic Books, 2010.

7. Specialty Coffee Association (SCA). *Coffee Standards and Glossary.* Long Beach, CA: SCA. https://sca.coffee/research.

8. Weinberg, Bennett Alan, and Bonnie K. Bealer. *The World of Caffeine: The Science and Culture of the World's Most Popular Drug.* New York: Routledge, 2002.

9. Wild, Antony. *Coffee: A Dark History.* New York: W. W. Norton & Company, 2005.

10. Wintgens, Jean Nicolas, ed. *Coffee: Growing, Processing, Sustainable Production – A Guidebook for Growers, Processors, Traders, and Researchers.* 2nd ed. Weinheim: Wiley-VCH, 2009.

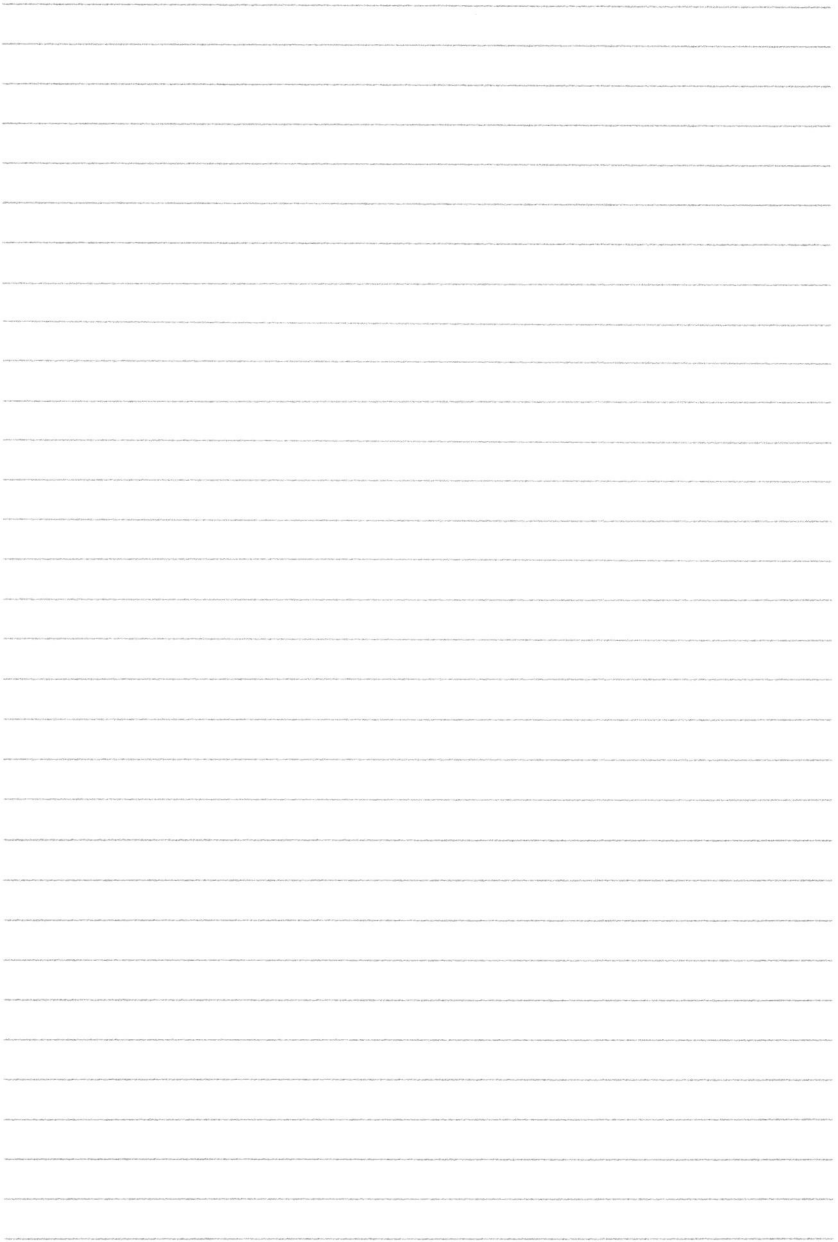

ABOUT THE AUTHOR

Lucas Almonte, Esq., is a first-generation Dominican-American born and raised in Manhattan, New York. He currently lives in Brooklyn, New York, and is a licensed attorney in the State of New York.

Lucas is the co-founder of Uplift NYC, a New York City–based 501(c)(3) tax-exempt organization dedicated to providing low-income youth and their families with access to critical educational, health, cultural, and legal aid resources and programs.

A lifelong learner, Lucas pursues a wide range of passions, including astronomy, chess, cooking, cycling, home gardening, painting, photography, and traveling (having explored over 30 countries and counting). He also finds joy in pouring latte art and shares his creations on Instagram and TikTok (@LatteArtByLucas). He owns two telescopes and is a member of the Amateur Astronomers Association in New York.

An avid sports enthusiast, Lucas played baseball, basketball, bowling, soccer, and American football at various levels of competition growing up. He is both a certified agent of the National Basketball Players Association (NBPA) and a licensed agent of the *Fédération Internationale de Basketball* (FIBA).

Lucas holds a Juris Doctor (J.D.) from Georgetown University Law Center and a Bachelor of Science (B.S.) from New York City College of Technology – City University of New York (CUNY).

SCAN THE QR CODE BELOW TO:

- Purchase the book
- Leave a review on Amazon.com
- Follow us on social media
- Visit our website

THANK YOU!

www.ingramcontent.com/pod-product-compliance
Lightning Source LLC
Chambersburg PA
CBHW051844040426
42447CB00006B/688